CONTENTS

MUCKY MONSTERS!

GET READY TO MEET THE TERRIFYING FOUR-EYED OGGLEMONSTER AND HIS HORRIBLE GOBBLE GANG!

ODDBALL

With three legs, this little monster hops around at top speed causing lots of mischief! He loves playing hide and surprise!

SLUDGER

Just one touch of Sludger's foul-smelling, toxic slime is enough to turn your skin green! He lives in a deep, dark swamp.

4

DRAW HORRIBLE STUFF

ARCTURUS

This edition published in 2012 by Arcturus Publishing Limited
26/27 Bickels Yard, 151–153 Bermondsey Street,
London SE1 3HA

ISBN: 978-1-84858-423-5
CH002147EN

Illustrated by Paul Gamble
Designed by Gary Sutherland
Edited by Anna Brett

Supplier 05, Date 0612, Print Run 1624

Printed in Singapore

GOB

This monster just can't keep his giant jaws shut and is always spraying spit all over the place! Don't ask him to say any terrible tongue twisters!

SQUIDRIP

Mind you don't get caught in these tentacles! Once Squidrip gets hold of something, he won't let go... unless you tickle him, of course!

BOGEY GREMLIN

Don't let this cute face fool you. This monster has the most horrible habits going. Picking his nose, farting and burping are some of his favourite things!

DRAW ME iF YOU DARE!

Remember to press softly so you can erase any mistakes.

1. The Ogglemonster starts life as a rectangle with a slight wobble to it.

2. Add two triangle shaped ears to the top of the body. An arch separates his two legs.

3. One, two, three, four eyes and mouth! Erase any original lines you no longer need.

4. Give our friend some arms. One curves up, the other curves down. Maybe he's doing a dance?

5. Add two toothy tusks and some fingers. Not so friendly anymore!

6. Now for the finishing touches – claws, boils, pupils and some goop! Ogglemonster complete!

Now add colour! Is that mud or slime?

DOODLE THIS TRICKSTER!

1. To start Oddball, draw a slightly squashed circle with a wiggly tail.

2. Add curved lines where his horns and three legs are going to be.

3. Draw in Oddball's stinky feet, pointy horns and add arms. Give him a proper tail, too.

He hops like me!

4. Draw in the rest of his legs and add his first eye. Did you notice Oddball only has two toes on each foot?

5. Give him fingers and two more eyes. Add the warts on his tail and draw his open mouth.

Erase your rough lines as you go along.

6. Finish Oddball by filling in his mouth, adding pupils and movement lines around his body. Where's he off to?

1. To create Sludger's shape, draw three squashed circles overlapping each other.

2. Start his horrible face with eyeballs and a large mouth.

3. Use the eyebrows to make him look mean. Give him big, thick arms too.

BRING ON THE SLIME!

Friendly looking guy, isn't he?!

10

4. Draw in his deadly slime bucket and the fingers on his left hand. Add pupils to his savage stare!

5. Finish drawing the bucket and his hands. Now let's add some slime!

6. Fill in his mouth and eyes, then go slime crazy! Make him as gloopy and horrible as you can!

What colour is he going to be?

LIZARDMAN IS UP TO HIS OLD TRICKS, DOODLE WHO HE'S ABOUT TO SPLAT!

14

UMBRELLA AT THE READY!

1. Start drawing Gob by placing one small oval above a larger one.

2. Join the ovals together with some curved lines to create Gob's huge mouth. Then add some big eyeballs.

3. Gob's lower lip is huge! Draw a nice big rectangle for it.

4. Rub out any lines you don't need and join up Gob's mouth and lip. Draw the outlines of his hands and feet, and add an X for his tie.

See Gob in action at the School of Monsters on page 22!

5. Mark where his hair will be. Add in pupils and a floppy tongue. Draw his goofy teeth, fingers and toes.

6. To finish Gob tidy up your lines and shade inside his massive mouth. Don't forget to add that horrible flying spit!

Who's a pretty boy then?

EVEN i THiNK HE'S DiSGUSTiNG!

1. Our mini friend, the Bogey Gremlin, starts out as a pear shape topped with a squashed circle.

2. Draw the outlines of his hands and feet. Careful with the positioning as we're drawing him side on.

3. Erase any rough lines. Then give him pointy ears and draw in his arms.

4. Draw his legs, toes, fingers and horns. Put a big curved line in where his mouth will be. He looks quite cute at the moment!

5. Add fluff to his ears, then give him eyes and teeth. He's not so cute now he's picking his nose!

6. Now to finish him off. Cover him in fur, draw in his tie and you are done!

Movement lines show he's waving.

19

THE MEANEST IN THE GANG

1. To start Squidrip, you need to draw two egg-shaped ovals overlapping each other – one large, one small.

2. Draw circles for his eyes in the smaller oval and a wobbly line for his mouth in the larger oval.

3. Pencil in the top of his mouth and the line across his eyes where his brow will be. Then add two swirly lines for his tentacles.

What is a monster's favourite game? Swallow the leader!

He doesn't look very scary yet!

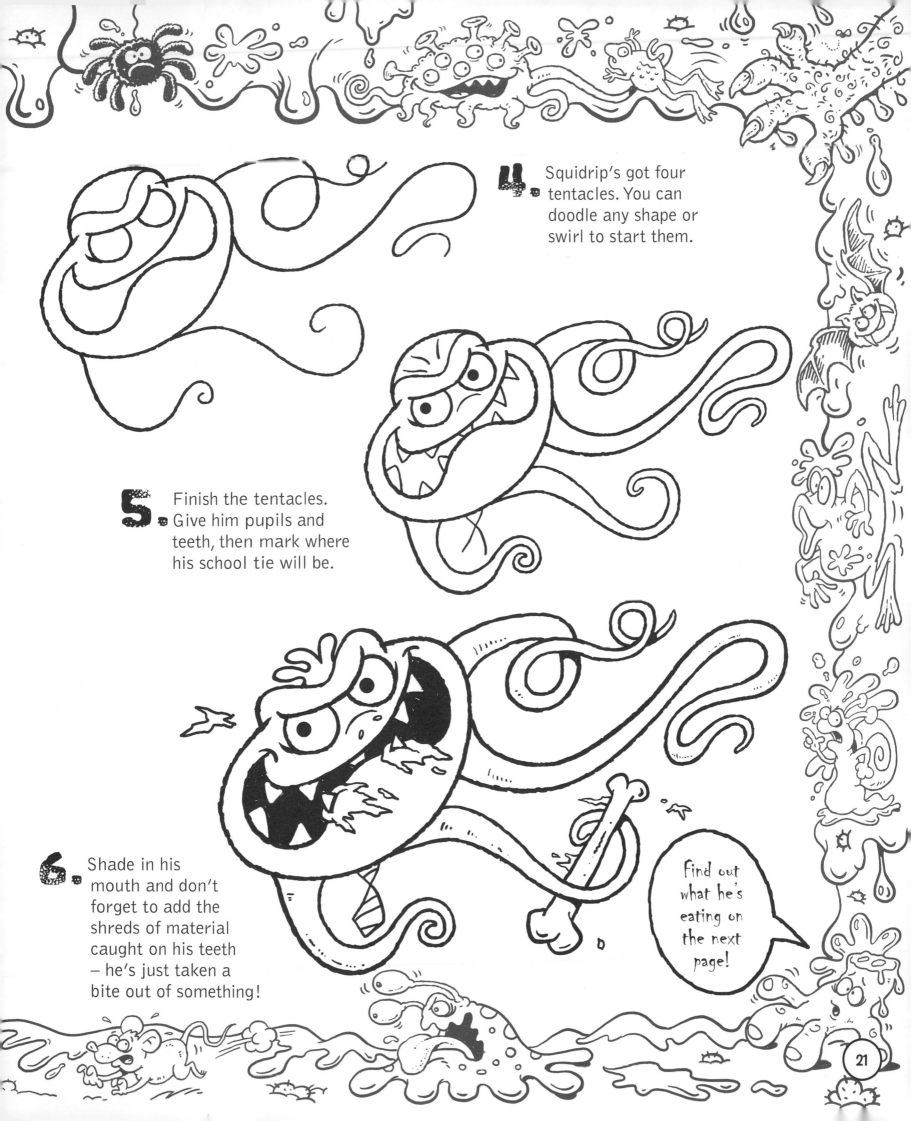

4. Squidrip's got four tentacles. You can doodle any shape or swirl to start them.

5. Finish the tentacles. Give him pupils and teeth, then mark where his school tie will be.

6. Shade in his mouth and don't forget to add the shreds of material caught on his teeth – he's just taken a bite out of something!

Find out what he's eating on the next page!

WHAT GRAFFITI ARTWORK HAS THIS TROUBLESOME PAIR PAINTED?

CREEPY CRAWLIES!

HARRY HORNET AND THE CRAWLY GANG WILL EAT ANYTHING — MOULDY FOOD, ROTTEN RUBBISH AND EVEN HUMAN TOENAILS!

RAVENOUS RUTH

Ruth's got twenty legs and a long body to fill with food, so she's always got her fork at the ready for the next snack. Her favourite food is rotten cabbage!

SNOT

Snot oozes, drips and slops slime everywhere! You can always spot where he's been because he leaves a sticky, grey trail behind him. Don't touch it, though, or you'll get stuck!

SQUIRMY

Squirmy the worm is a crafty chap. He wriggles around, in and out of the ground, dodging birds and hoarding all the best food for himself! His underground lair is huge!

SQUELCH

This naughty little spider is nicknamed after his favourite noise. He loves it when he bites into his prey and it goes SQUELCH! His webs are the best in the business, there's no escape once you're caught.

GUZZLETUM

He is the fattest, meanest, greenest toad in the swamp! He lurks behind the lilies, pouncing on unsuspecting flies and belches after every mouthful!

I'M COMING TO STING YOU!

1. Harry Hornet has an oval shaped body. The fatter end will be his head, so decide what direction you want him to face.

2. Add two wings on top of his body, notice how the back one goes behind the body. Add his pointed stinger and nose.

3. Draw in a huge eye and a zigzag line for his mouth. You can erase the lines across his wings and nose now.

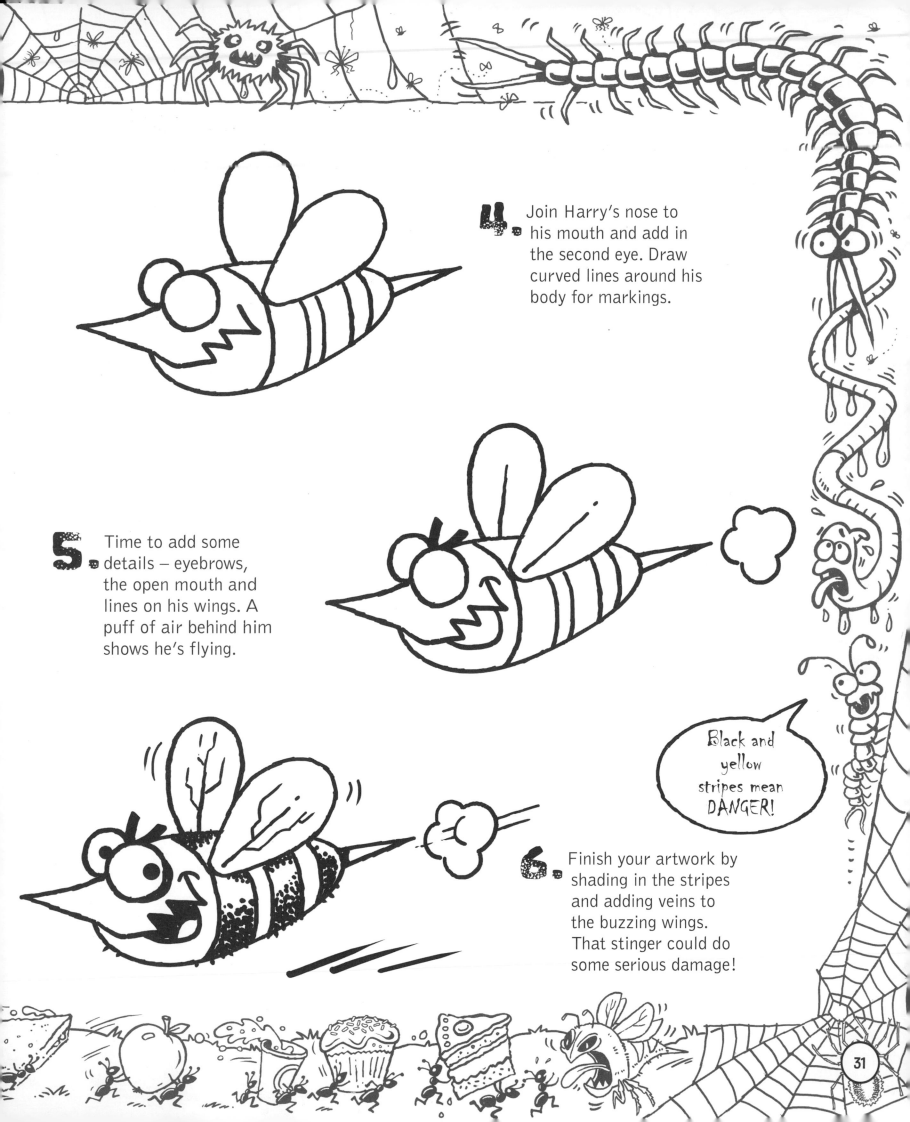

4. Join Harry's nose to his mouth and add in the second eye. Draw curved lines around his body for markings.

5. Time to add some details – eyebrows, the open mouth and lines on his wings. A puff of air behind him shows he's flying.

Black and yellow stripes mean DANGER!

6. Finish your artwork by shading in the stripes and adding veins to the buzzing wings. That stinger could do some serious damage!

KEEP CLEAR OF THAT FORK!

1. This creepy caterpillar, Ravenous Ruth, starts out as an oval at the end of a wiggly line. She looks like a tadpole at the moment!

2. Begin to build up her body by drawing lots of ovals stacked on top of each other.

3. Continue drawing ovals until you have ten in total. Then add some googly eyeballs. Now she's starting to look like a caterpillar!

4. Draw some patches on each segment of her body, and add arms and a smile. Erase any rough lines.

She hasn't got as many legs as me!

5. To make her truly horrible add hair everywhere, goofy teeth and a long tongue.

6. Finish Ruth off by adding her feet, pupils and antennae. With her fork in hand she's ready to feast!

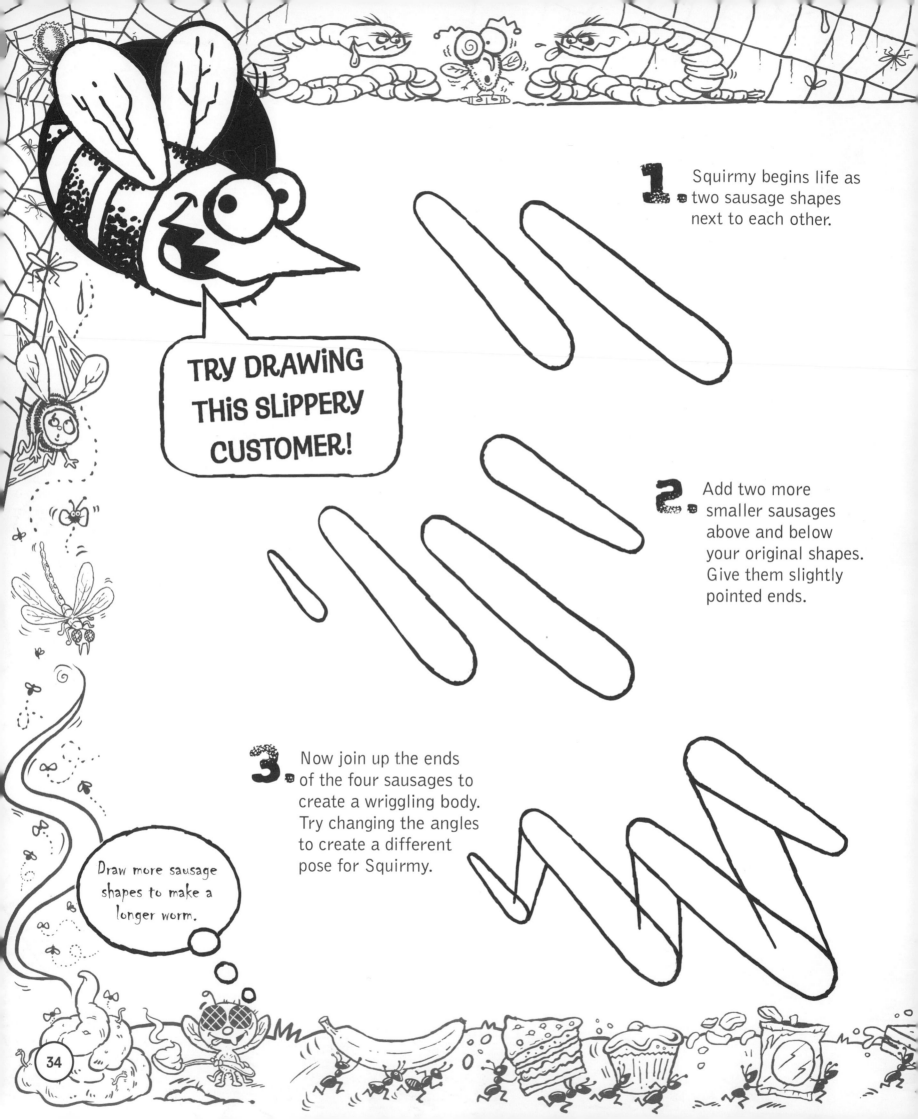

1. Squirmy begins life as two sausage shapes next to each other.

2. Add two more smaller sausages above and below your original shapes. Give them slightly pointed ends.

3. Now join up the ends of the four sausages to create a wriggling body. Try changing the angles to create a different pose for Squirmy.

Draw more sausage shapes to make a longer worm.

34

4. Rub out the lines so Squirmy's body is one single shape. Now add the outlines for his turned-up nose, open mouth and one eye.

5. Draw in his second eye, using the first for positioning. Add two lines across his back for the saddle – that's the darker stripe on a worm's body.

6. Pointed eyebrows and a shadow around his eye make him look cunning. Movement lines show he's in a hurry to hunt down some grub!

CRISPY GNATS

DRAW THE YUCKY FILLINGS IN A BUG BAGUETTE!

BANANA SKINS

BLOOD KETCHUP

CRUNCHY SNAIL SHELLS

DUNG PÂTÉ

WORM CHEESE

MUD SPRINKLES
TO SEASON

ROTTEN
TOMATOES

PLEASED TO EAT YOU!

1. Start with an easy circle for Squelch's body. How large are you going to draw him?

2. Add eight lines sticking out of the circle for his legs. Count to make sure you've got them all.

3. Now make the legs rounded and add two eyeballs. Spiders actually have eight eyes, so you could add another six to your drawing!

4. Time to transform him into the naughty spider he really is! Give him angry eyebrows and a wide mouth. Draw in a jagged line around his body.

5. A furry body and fangs make this a spider to steer clear of. Outline his tongue, too.

6. To finish Squelch, give him pupils and shade around his eyes. Add some hairs on his legs and then colour him in – black, blue or maybe orange?

This way little ants! It's feeding time!

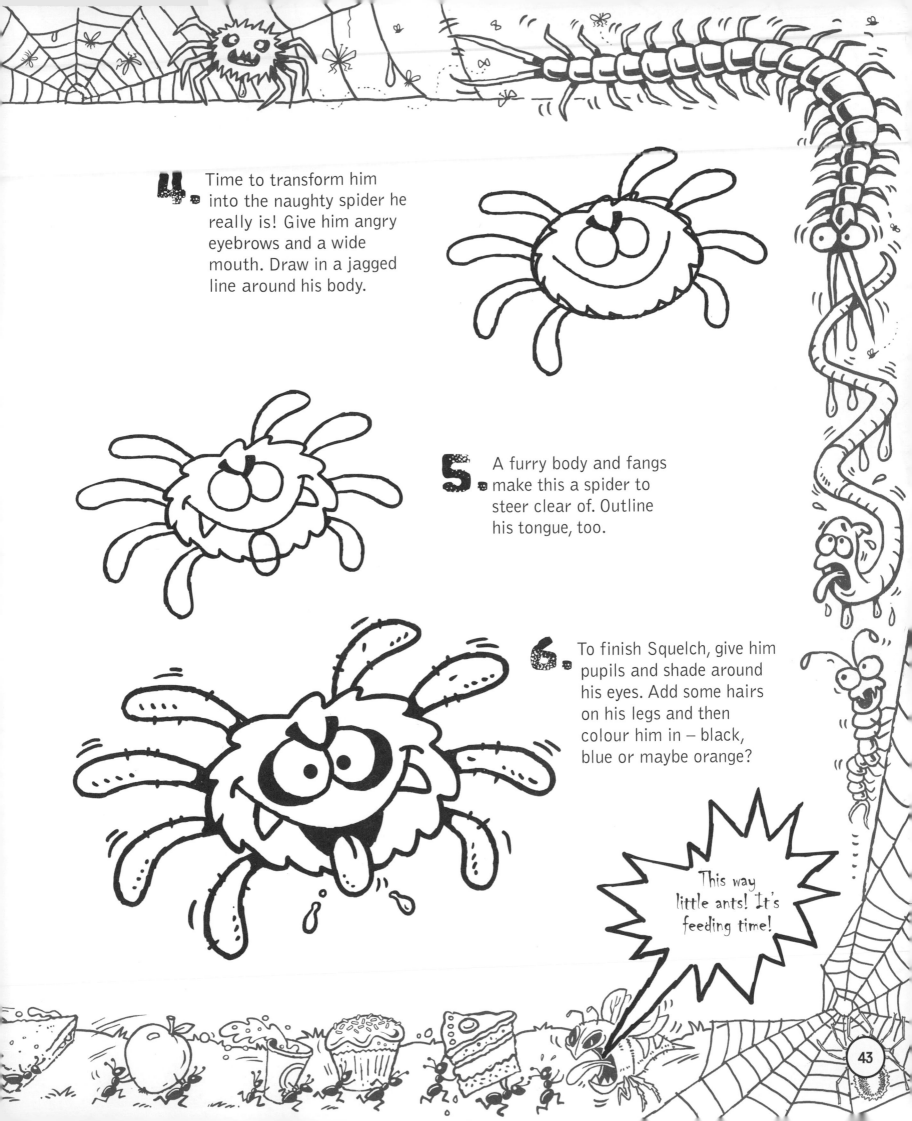

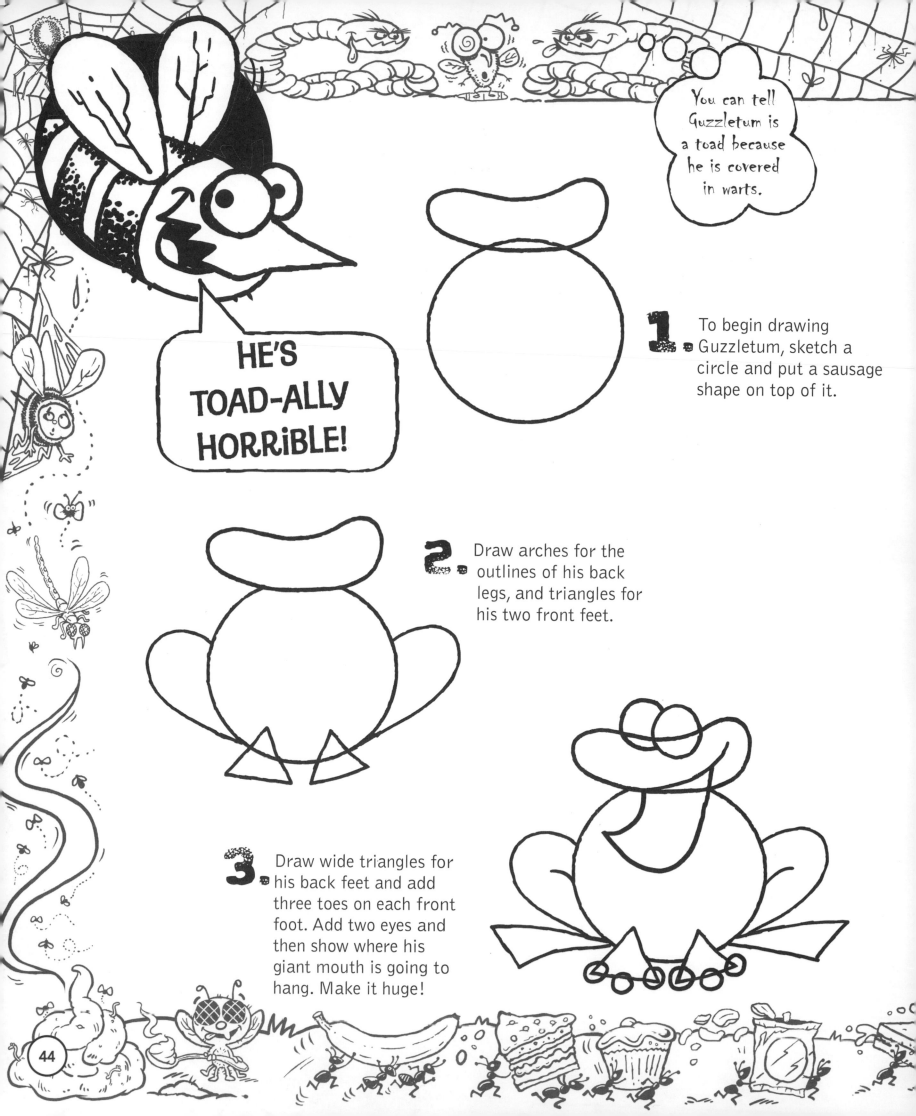

HE'S TOAD-ALLY HORRIBLE!

You can tell Guzzletum is a toad because he is covered in warts.

1. To begin drawing Guzzletum, sketch a circle and put a sausage shape on top of it.

2. Draw arches for the outlines of his back legs, and triangles for his two front feet.

3. Draw wide triangles for his back feet and add three toes on each front foot. Add two eyes and then show where his giant mouth is going to hang. Make it huge!

44

4. Add toes on the back feet and then shape his mouth. I wonder how many flies he has swallowed today?

5. Now draw his long, sticky tongue flying out to catch prey. Give him some angry eyebrows, too.

6. Finish Guzzletum by adding lots of warts and his pupils. Don't forget to draw the poor fly!

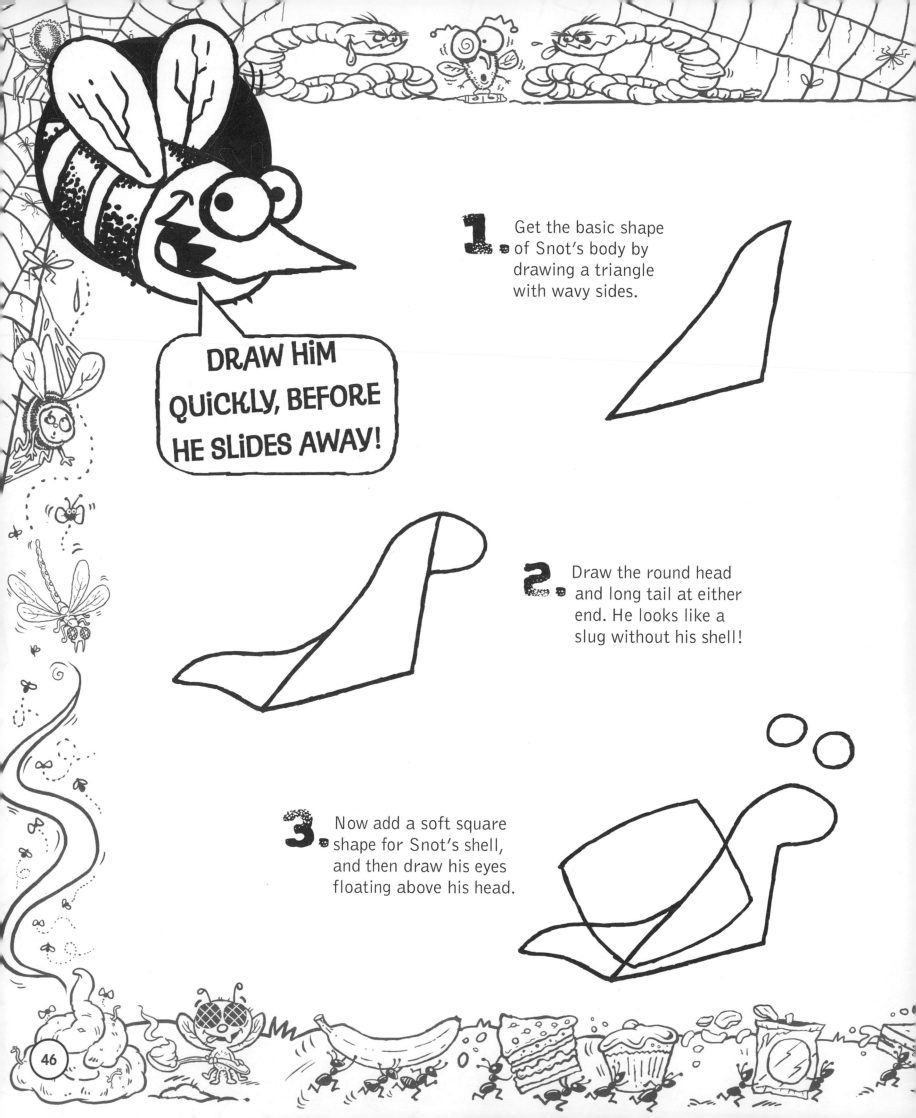

DRAW HiM QUiCKLY, BEFORE HE SLiDES AWAY!

1. Get the basic shape of Snot's body by drawing a triangle with wavy sides.

2. Draw the round head and long tail at either end. He looks like a slug without his shell!

3. Now add a soft square shape for Snot's shell, and then draw his eyes floating above his head.

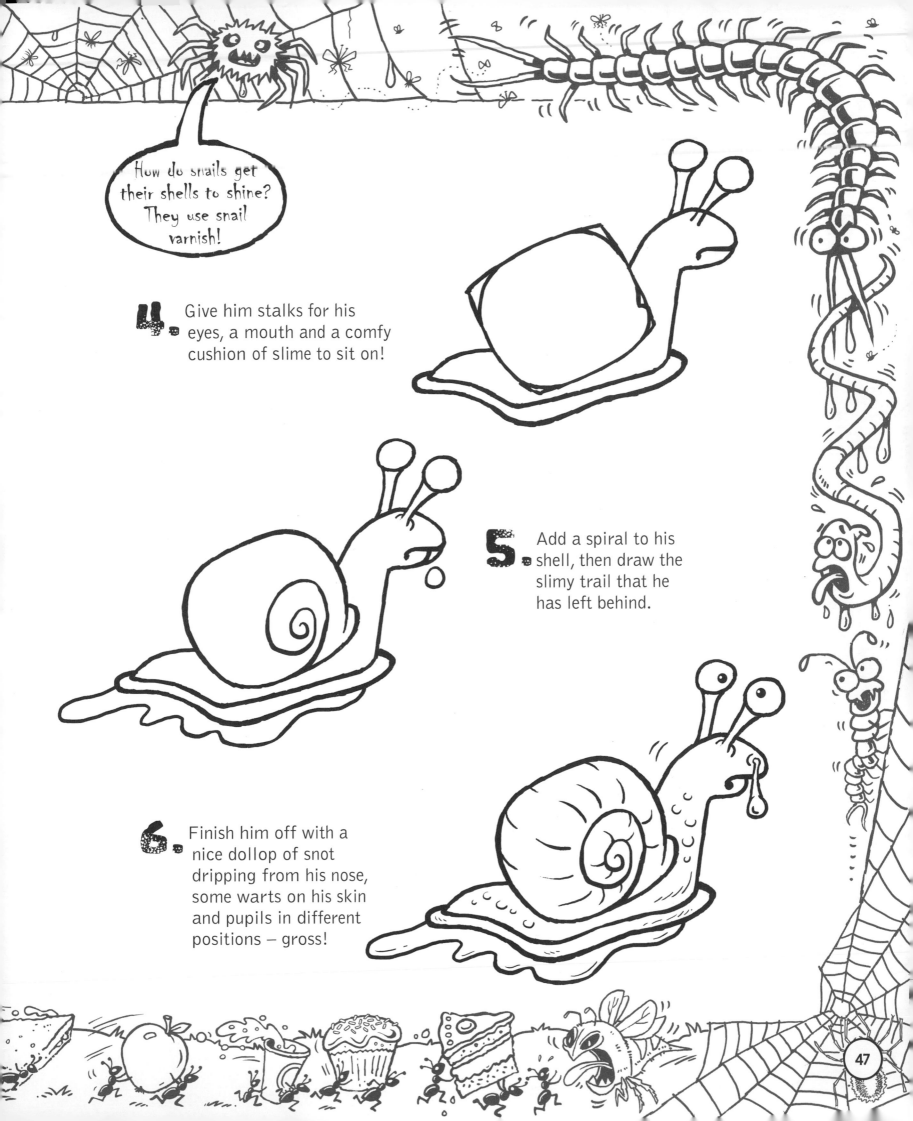

How do snails get their shells to shine? They use snail varnish!

4. Give him stalks for his eyes, a mouth and a comfy cushion of slime to sit on!

5. Add a spiral to his shell, then draw the slimy trail that he has left behind.

6. Finish him off with a nice dollop of snot dripping from his nose, some warts on his skin and pupils in different positions – gross!

WHAT ELSE HAS THIS SPIDER GOT FOR DINNER?

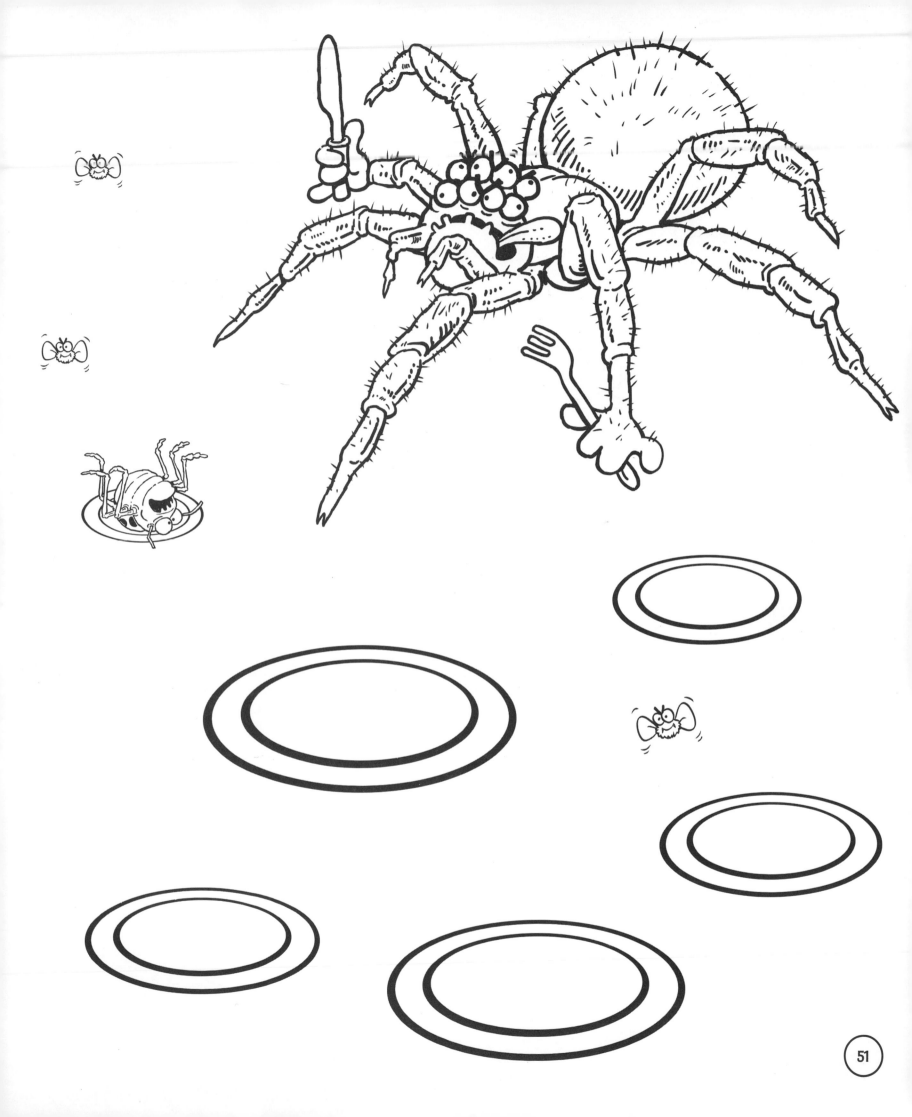

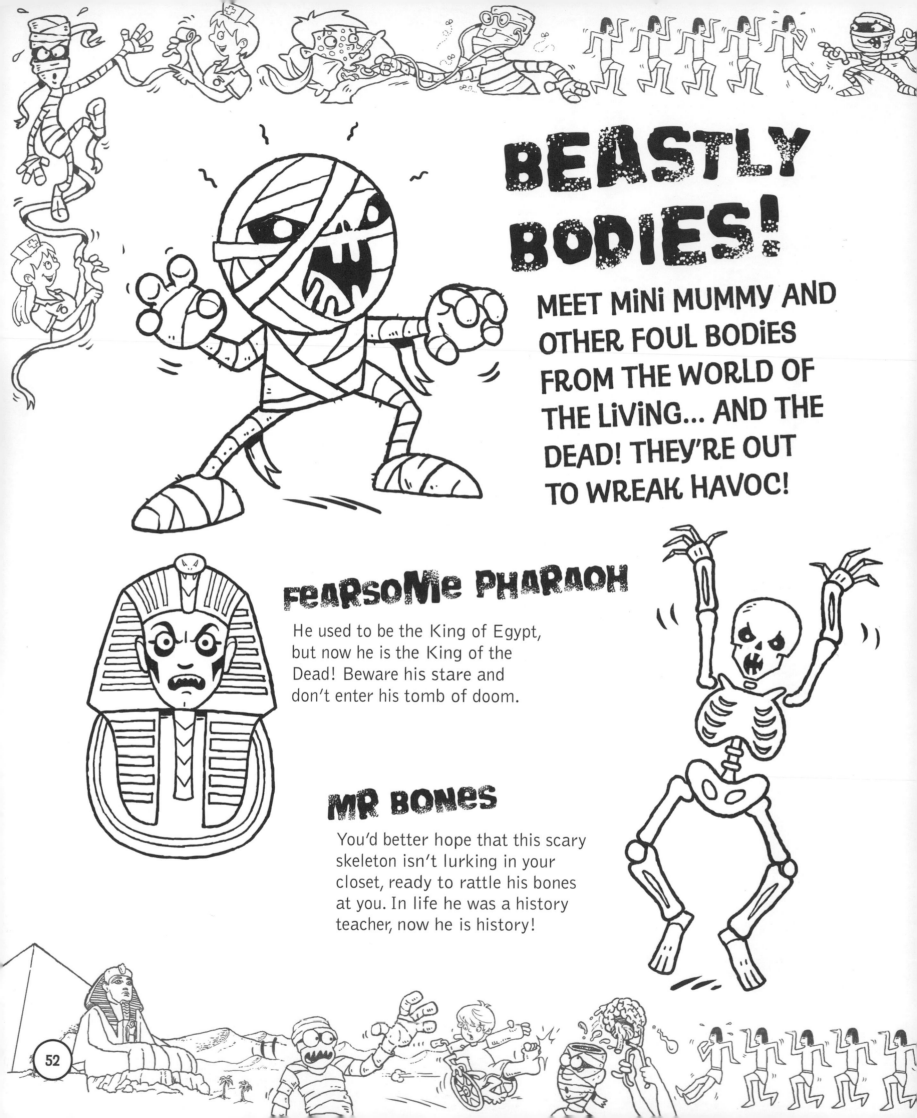

BEASTLY BODIES!

MEET MINI MUMMY AND OTHER FOUL BODIES FROM THE WORLD OF THE LIVING... AND THE DEAD! THEY'RE OUT TO WREAK HAVOC!

FEARSOME PHARAOH

He used to be the King of Egypt, but now he is the King of the Dead! Beware his stare and don't enter his tomb of doom.

MR BONES

You'd better hope that this scary skeleton isn't lurking in your closet, ready to rattle his bones at you. In life he was a history teacher, now he is history!

VOMITING VICTOR

Ever since he was dared to eat some frog's legs, Victor has become a human vomit fountain! No one knows when he'll stop, or who will clear up the trail of slop!

SNEEZY LUIGI

When Luigi sneezes it's like a fireworks display. High-speed snot rockets out of his nose every few minutes, in a variety of colours!

ZACHARY

Poor baby Zachary is covered with horrible itchy boils and scabs. The pox is just part of the problem, though, as Zachary catches every illness going!

GOT THIS DRAWING ALL WRAPPED UP?

The smell of rotting bandages makes me feel sick!

1. Start Mini Mummy by drawing a large circle and then adding a small rectangle for his body.

2. Draw two small circles where the hands will be, and then two ovals for the feet.

3. Sketch in his arms and Mini Mummy begins to take shape. You can add the open mouth now, too.

4. Flesh out the arms and legs, adding four fingers. Then work on his evil face.

5. Add some pupils and gappy teeth. Then start to draw lines where his bandages are.

6. Finish off Mini Mummy by filling his eyes and mouth in black. Draw the rest of his bandages and leave two small holes for his nose.

I'm 7000 years old!

THIS IS JUST A MASK, HIS FACE IS WORSE!

1. Begin by drawing two curved shapes for this fearsome Pharaoh's headdress and neck plate.

2. Next, add a curve where the Pharaoh's head is going to be, and two shapes to mark the bottom of the headdress.

3. Draw a curved line to mark the top of his head and put in the outline of the snake on his crown. You can also draw in his long beard.

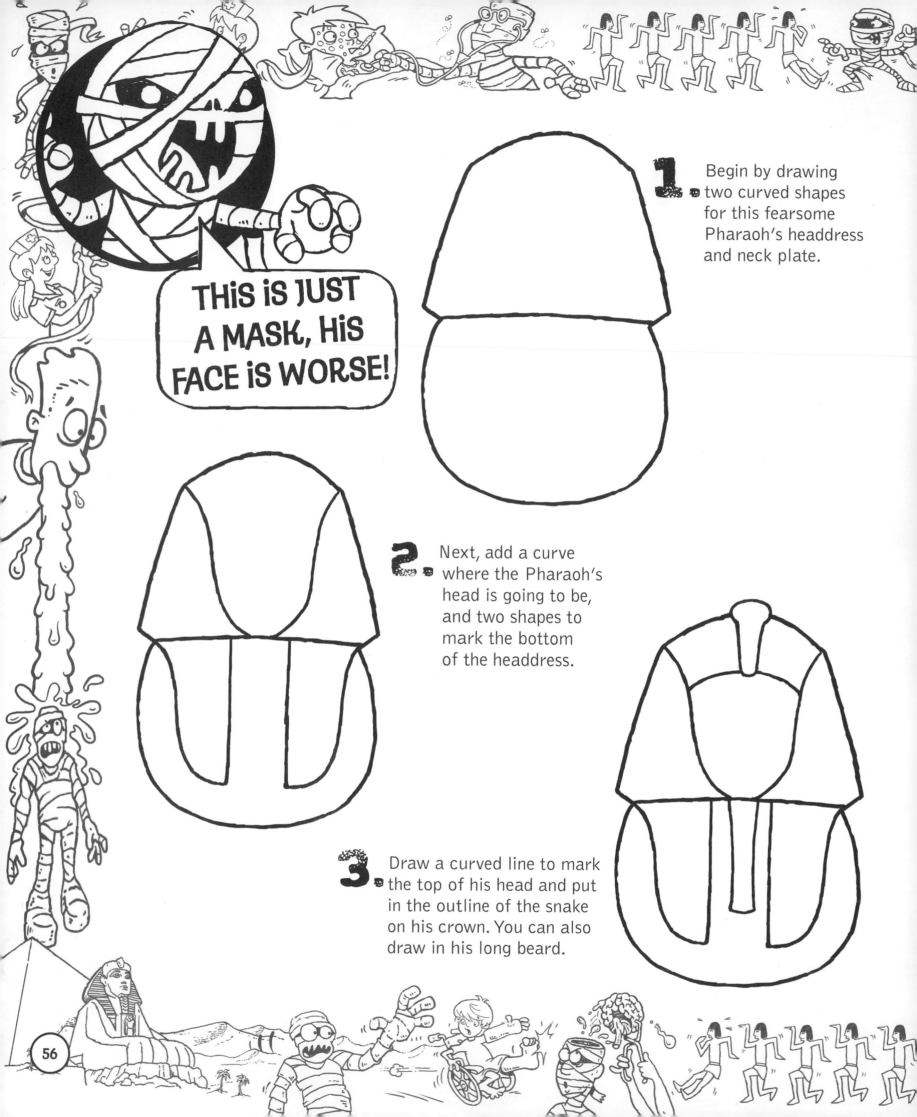

4. Add two lines around the bottom of the neck plate, then give the King his ears, eyes and mouth. Add in the sneering snake's eyes and nose.

5. Add the stripes on the headdress and plait the beard. Give this Pharaoh big eyebrows, eyeliner, fangs and markings on his cheeks.

6. Add pupils, a furrowed brow and some shading to finish your majestic portrait. Colour it in regal gold and royal blue!

I hear mummies like listening to wrap music best!

SKETCH THESE RATTLING BONES!

1. Start Mr Bones by drawing a semicircle where his head will be, and two kidney shapes for his ribs and hips.

2. Add in his triangular jaw, and bones for the top of his arms and legs. Practise drawing the classic bone shape.

3. Draw in the rest of the arms and legs, paying attention to his pose. Then draw small rectangles where his spine will be.

4. Mr Bones does not enjoy being dead so give him angry eyes! Add small shapes for all his joints.

The thigh bone's connected to the hip bone, the hip bone's connected...

5. Draw pupils and a mouth. Then add fingers, toes, ribs and splits in his arm and leg bones.

6. Add the finishing touches to Mr Bones as shown in the picture and you're done. He's after all those pupils who haven't done their history homework!

SOMETHING HAS FRIGHTENED THIS ARCHAEOLOGIST. DRAW WHAT HE CAN SEE INSIDE THE PYRAMID.

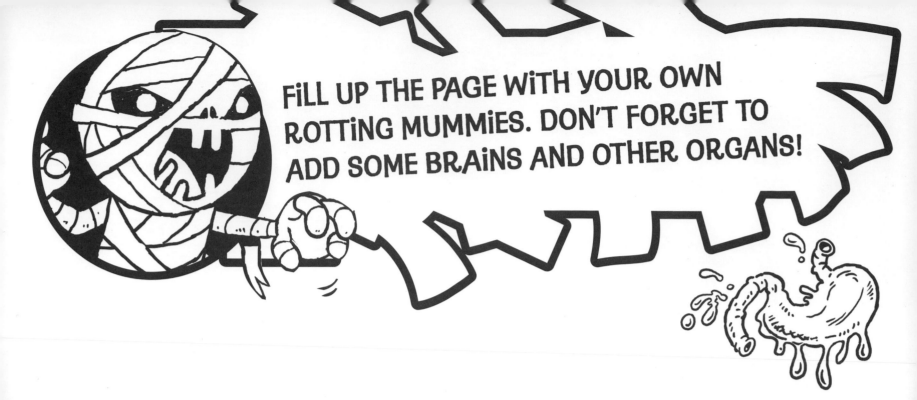

FILL UP THE PAGE WITH YOUR OWN ROTTING MUMMIES. DON'T FORGET TO ADD SOME BRAINS AND OTHER ORGANS!

65

iT'S THE HUMAN VOM-CANO!

1. Before Victor starts vomiting he begins life as a soft-cornered rectangle connected to a curved body shape.

2. Add another curved shape for his legs, and then two circles where his hands will be.

3. Draw the outline of his open mouth, his left arm, the fingers on his left hand and his feet.

You could change Victor into Vicky!

4. Finish his fingers and add eyeballs and legs. Then draw the stream of vomit, it's as thick as one of his legs!

5. Make a nice puddle of vomit on the floor. Yuck! Then draw a nose, hair and some large bags under Victor's eyes – being sick is tiring work!

6. Give Victor some pupils and eyebrows, then make his vomit as horrible as you can! Why not draw in what he ate for his last meal!

HE'S WORSE THAN THE BOGEYMAN!

1. Draw a circle and then attach the rectangular shape of Luigi's torso to it.

2. Draw the outline of his bent legs, his tissue and a circle where his hand is going to be.

Use soft but clean lines to draw your guides. This makes them easier to erase.

3. Add some arms and feet. He's got bent legs to show the force of his sneeze!

Get ready for the snot explosion!

4. Divide his legs in two, give him some fingers and an ear. Then outline his t-shirt, hair and tissue.

5. Add in some more detail to the t-shirt and his hair, then draw triangles for your snot guidelines!

6. Finally, add extra wrinkles around Luigi's eyes to show they're squeezed shut. Make the flying snot as gross as you can!

POP THOSE POX!

1. Start by drawing a triangle with a circle sitting on top. This will help you get Zachary's proportions right.

2. Within the triangle, draw a egg for the body, beans for the feet and sausages for the arms. Making you hungry?

3. Add circles where his hands will be. Then add legs and a big, wailing mouth.

4. Rub out the triangle guide. Now he's taking shape. Draw fingers, ears, closed eyes, one big tooth and a tongue.

5. Time to add detail! Add buttons and cuffs to his babygrow, then concentrate on his face.

He thinks HE has a problem? Look at me!

6. To finish Zachary, give him lots of nasty spots all over his face. Tears and movement lines show he is screaming!

FILL UP THIS HORRIBLE WAITING ROOM WITH YOUR OWN PUTRID PATIENTS. WHAT GHASTLY SYMPTOMS HAVE THEY GOT?

HORRID HORRORS!

THIS GANG OF GHOULS ARE LED BY VAMPELLA. HER TEETH ARE THE SHARPEST IN THE BUSINESS.

SID THE SPIRIT

This mischievous spirit is out to have fun. He's top of the shocks and loves to spook little kids and puppy dogs.

PUTRID PETE

Pete's stench is enough to make you puke! He's an expert at the zombie shuffle, especially with his decaying limbs.

WILD MAUD

Maud is as ugly on the inside as she is on the outside. Beware her broth, it'll turn your face green and your nails black!

BLACK WING

This chap is Vampella's right hand bat. He's got an amazing sense of smell, so needs to avoid flying into Putrid Pete!

DRACO JUNIOR

Don't be fooled by Draco's good looks, he's the most feared creature of the night... and has a very famous father!

DRAW SID AND SCARE YOUR FRIENDS!

1. Sid starts life as a curved rectangle. Easy!

2. His arms are up in the air and shaped like bananas. Spirits don't have legs, so make the bottom of the rectangle ragged.

Try drawing me too!

3. Add circles for hands, a curve at the back of his head and some more tatters at the bottom.

4. Sid's clawed hands make up for his lack of legs! Now's the time to add a wicked grin.

5. Give him evil eyes by drawing little semicircles. His jagged teeth are just mini triangles.

6. Sid's in fright mode so add some movement lines around his body. Shade around his eyes and his jagged bottom.

MAUD'S NOTHING BUT TROUBLE!

What is a witch's favourite subject at school? Spelling!

1. Begin with a shape like a witch's hat. It's a triangle with a longer bottom side.

2. Draw a circle inside the triangle, and add two pointy arms on either side.

3. Three additions at this stage – a circle around her head, a line for the bottom of her dress and a V shape for the broom.

4. Get your eraser out and suddenly Maud begins to take shape. Draw in her feet, face, hands and hair.

5. The tip of her hat is bent, much like her large nose! Draw it in, along with her eyelids and open mouth.

6. The finishing touches include lots of warts! She's got a single tooth and wicked eyes. Watch her fly into the night to cause mischief!

PUTRID PETE'S A PICTURE!

1. A bell or a pear? This is how Pete starts life. You could even try to draw a whole zombie army.

2. Add a circle for the head and two ovals for his feet.

Is that cheese I can smell?

3. Draw a triangle between his feet to get the shape of his legs. Two circles will become his hands.

4. Add circles for his eyes, a bean-shaped mouth, tattered trouser legs and zombie arms.

5. I don't think a dentist would be happy with Pete's teeth, even his floppy tongue is trying to avoid them!

6. Now add the details – pupils, shadows under his eyes, ragged clothes and drops of slop!

85

BROTH RECIPE

 1 SQUEEZE OF SLUG'S SLIME

10 NEWTS' EYES

3 FROGS' LEGS

1 BAT'S WING

4 SPIDERS AND THEIR WEBS

THE BONES OF A WOLF

1 CHICKEN'S FOOT

1 WHOLE OCTOPUS

OOOH! DON'T i LOOK GOOD!

I hope I look this good when i'm 208 years old!

1. To draw Vampella, start with a circle connected to a long bell shape.

2. Add carrot shapes for feet and circles for hands. She's got pointed pixie ears.

3. Sketch in the outline of Vampella's long hair, then add her arms and legs.

4. Draw in her wicked pointy fingers and make the bottom of her dress ragged, she's been wearing it for over 200 years!

5. Finish her flowing hair to show she's flying, and don't forget those fearsome fangs.

6. Add dark shadows under her eyes, and sloping eyebrows to give her a cunning look. Vamp-tastic!

FLY WITH BLACK WING

1. Black Wing begins life as a large triangle with a semicircle on top.

2. To get the shape of the wings, join the ends of the semicircle with the edges of the triangle. The little circle will be his head.

3. Erase the top of the triangle and add lines across the wings. Draw in his body.

4. You can draw in the proper wing shape now. Add his pointy ears, too.

5. Time to add a face and erase all the lines you no longer need.

Did you know bat wings are actually fingers joined up with skin!

6. Finish the wings and give him a furry body. Last but not least are his fangs, he is a vampire bat after all!

DRACO'S A DUDE!

1. Draco's no square, he's shaped like a rectangle! Add a circle at the top for his head.

2. Draw in a triangle for his body and two smaller circles for his hands.

3. Two triangles look like ears, but they're really the top of his cape!

4. Time to add some eyes and give the bottom of the cape a bat-wing shape.

5. Now draw in his pointy ears and fingers, and add his cheeky face!

6. Finally, add fangs and finishing touches. Colour him in with purple, red and black pencils.

I wonder what Dracula is up to these days?

WHO'S **SPOOKED** THE VAMPIRE SLAYER?

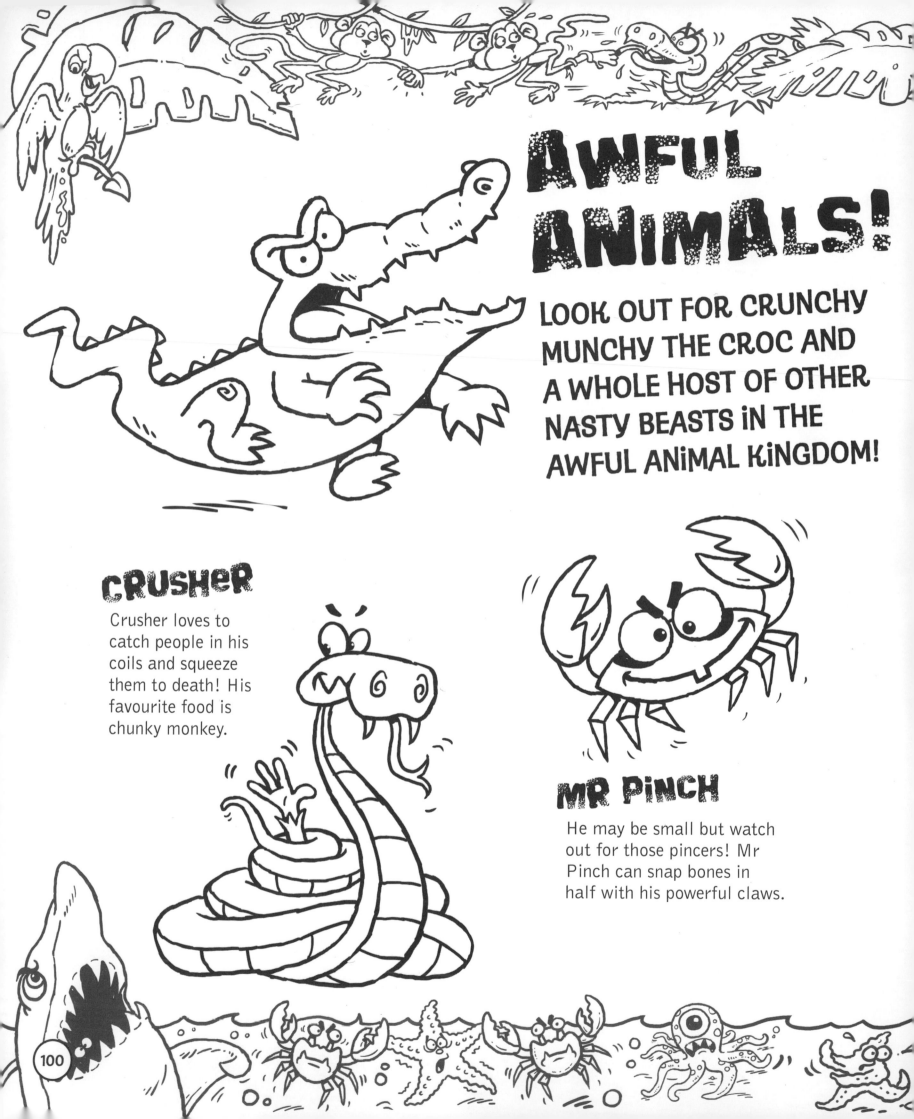

AWFUL ANIMALS!

LOOK OUT FOR CRUNCHY MUNCHY THE CROC AND A WHOLE HOST OF OTHER NASTY BEASTS IN THE AWFUL ANIMAL KINGDOM!

CRUSHER

Crusher loves to catch people in his coils and squeeze them to death! His favourite food is chunky monkey.

MR PINCH

He may be small but watch out for those pincers! Mr Pinch can snap bones in half with his powerful claws.

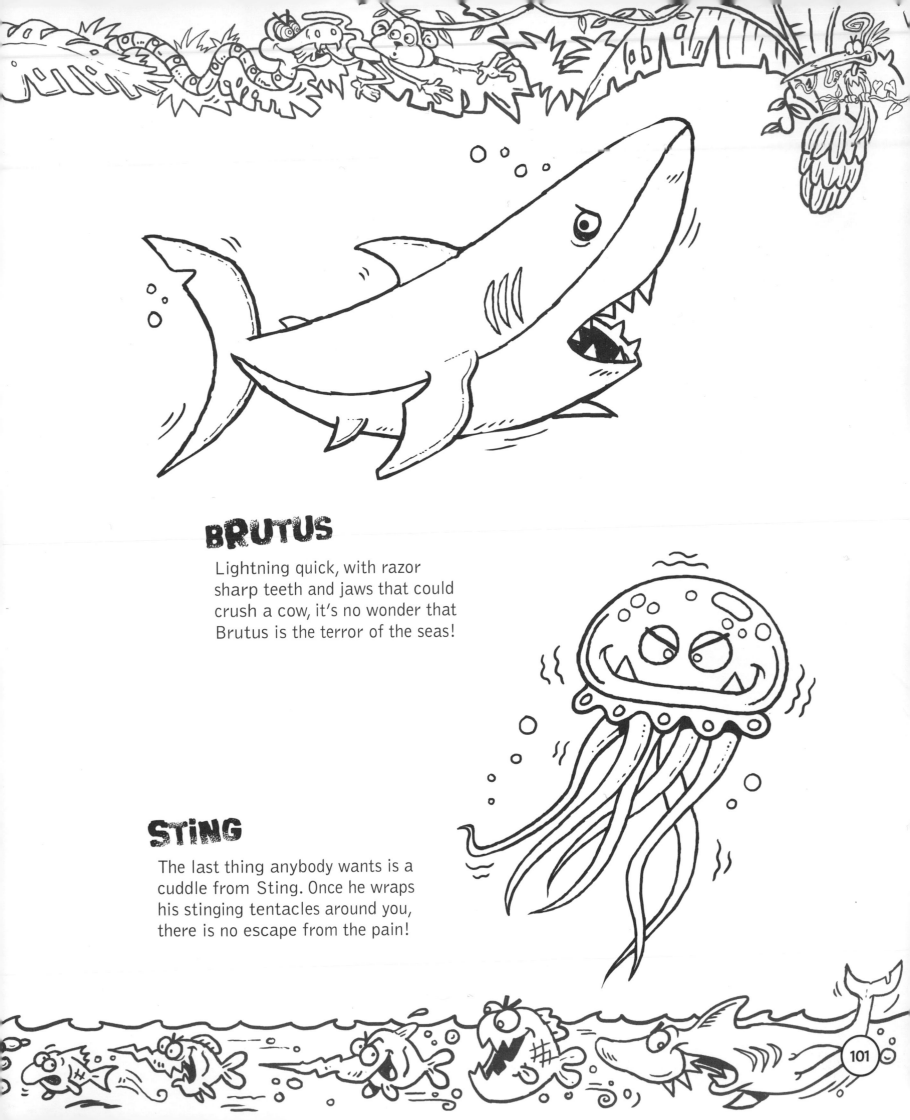

BRUTUS

Lightning quick, with razor
sharp teeth and jaws that could
crush a cow, it's no wonder that
Brutus is the terror of the seas!

STING

The last thing anybody wants is a
cuddle from Sting. Once he wraps
his stinging tentacles around you,
there is no escape from the pain!

i AM KiNG OF THE SWAMP!

1. First, draw a semicircle which will form the base of Crunchy Munchy's body.

2. Draw the outline of his head and a bean shape for the start of his tail. It doesn't look much like Crunchy yet...

3. Next, pencil in those snappy jaws. Draw the tip of his tail and four circles where his feet are going to be.

Never smile at a crocodile!

4. Time to draw in his legs and join up his tail. Erase the lines inside his mouth, then outline his eyes.

5. Crunchy Munchy needs angry eyebrows and claws to look scary. He's taking shape now!

6. Finish Crunchy with lots of spikes down his back and pointy teeth. Most crocs are green, but you can make Crunchy any colour you like!

HAVE A CUDDLE WITH CRUSHER

What kind of snake is good at maths? An adder!

1. Start with a long S shape for Crusher's body, and add a small round head.

2. Add his large rectangular jaw and the first coil in his squeezy trap!

3. Add a second coil and two eyes. Draw a line down his neck – this is where his back changes into his tummy.

4. Add a third coil and a wavy tongue. Add a circle to show where the monkey's hand is going to poke out.

5. Draw the final coil and finish the forked tongue. Add in the four-fingered monkey hand.

6. To finish Crusher, give him pupils, nostrils and fangs. Draw lines across his tummy and he's ready to eat his dinner!

SNIP SNAP!

1. Begin Mr Pinch the crab by drawing an oval leaf shape.

2. Draw two more leaf shapes above the first one. These will be the pincers.

I didn't think sharks liked jelly!

3. Add some arms to join the pincers to the body, two eyes and the tops of his legs. It looks like he is doing ballet!

4. Make the bottoms of his legs pointy, and then create his big pincers by drawing a lightning shape across the oval.

5. Thick eyebrows, shadows under his eyes and a creepy smile turn him from a regular crab into a cunning crustacean!

6. Mr Pinch is nearly ready – just add a single tooth and pupils and he is ready to scuttle off – sideways of course!

DRAW
BRUTAL
BRUTUS!

1. To draw Crunchy Munchy's mate Brutus, start off with a fat banana shape.

2. Draw a line down the middle to show where his belly will be, put a fin on his back and start the tail.

3. Add his smaller fins and mark where his gaping mouth is going to be. The tail is a quarter moon shape.

4. Draw in an eye and some gills. This is the last time Brutus is going to look friendly.

5. Give him angry eyes, pointy teeth and show where his tail has a battle scar from a fish fight.

6. To finish Brutus, shade the inside of his mouth, and around his eye, for an extra evil glare!

Stop that starfish!

THERE'S A STING IN HIS TAIL!

1. Start off with a curved semicircle. This will be Sting's large head.

2. Draw a wiggly frill across the bottom and add two round eyes.

3. Add the beginnings of the six tentacles. Make them wavy, like hair.

4. Finish off the thick tentacles and then draw a long, smiley mouth.

5. Time for the horrible bits! Give Sting some fangs and heavy eyelids.

6. Finish Sting off with shading, pupils, spots and bubbles to show he's underwater.

What colour will your jellyfish be?

SICKENING SCIENCE!

WELCOME TO DR STITCHUP'S CRAZY LABORATORY! NOTHING WILL STOP HIM IN HIS QUEST TO CREATE AN ARMY OF MONSTERS!

BONEHEAD

Bonehead has the most marvellous brain, which Dr S. is determined to preserve. He keeps him in a jar in his lab. Many of the most horrible experiments are Bonehead's idea.

IGOR

Every mad scientist needs a hunchbacked sidekick! They don't come more stupid than Igor, but he's handy for cleaning up blood and guts.

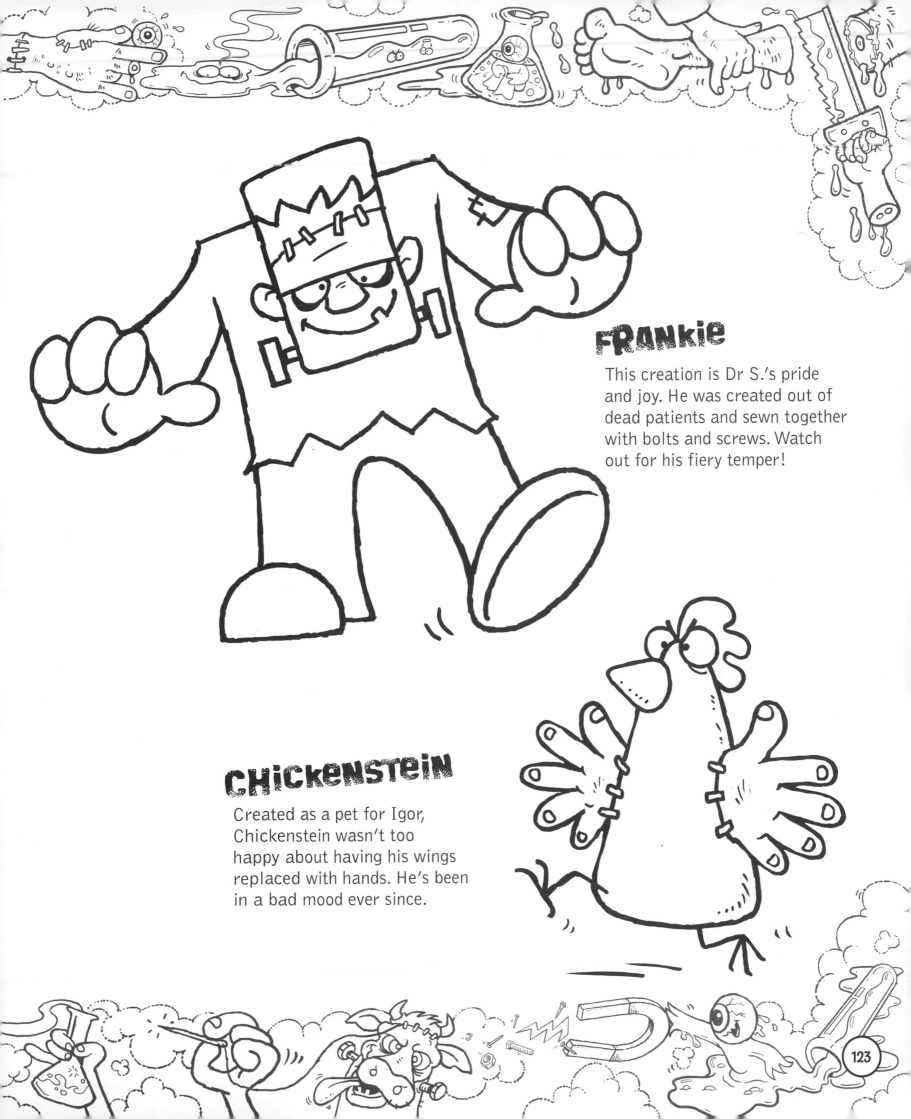

FRANKIE

This creation is Dr S.'s pride and joy. He was created out of dead patients and sewn together with bolts and screws. Watch out for his fiery temper!

CHICKENSTEIN

Created as a pet for Igor, Chickenstein wasn't too happy about having his wings replaced with hands. He's been in a bad mood ever since.

EUREKA!

1. Dr S. has a body shaped like a bell. His head and neck are long and thin, copy the odd shape!

2. Time to add arms and legs. If you start with a single line it's easier to get the shape right. He's got bent legs and raised arms.

3. Now add six circles. Two for the hands, two for the eyes and then one for his ear and collar.

4. Finish the hands and add a flask raised high in the air. All mad scientists need a pair of stupid specs and wild hair.

I said my leg was feeling a little sore!

5. Even though Dr S. is mad, he knows it's important to wear gloves when handling chemicals!

6. Finish his face with crazy eyes and make his hair frizzy. Add buttons down his lab coat and decide what potion he's brewing up!

1. Dr Stitchup's hunchbacked henchman begins life as an egg shape.

AHH, MY DEVOTED SERVANT, iGOR!

2. Add the circle for his head within the body shape, this creates the hunchback. He's got two little legs...

3. ... and feet shaped like beans. Add two round hands. Different sized eyes help make him look stupid.

Fishing with a magnet, that's a new trick!

4. Add in the arms and legs. It looks like he's hopping! His big smile extends beyond his eyes.

Igor's favourite soup is scream of tomato!

5. Give him a big goofy tongue and some ears. Draw on the rags he wears.

6. Igor's never been to the dentist and he's only got one tooth left. At least he doesn't need to worry about a hairdresser!

WHAT A HEAD CASE!

1. Begin by outlining Bonehead's skull. He doesn't have a body, so you can make it nice and large.

2. Draw two round eyes and a triangle for his nose hole — his nose fell off many years ago!

3. Give him a large grin and draw a line to divide off the top of his skull. Notice the wiggly line next to his eye, this forms the side of his face.

I wonder where Bonehead's body ended up?

4. Add stitches along the crack in the skull and some remaining teeth. Bonehead's sitting on a plate.

5. Erase the lines on the mouth you no longer need, add a curve around the eye, then draw in the bell jar.

6. Finally, add the details. Pupils, a black nose hole and some shine on the glass of the jar. A medical marvel!

My head hurts!

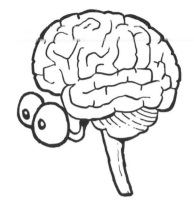

What other famous monsters can you think of?

MY BOY! HE'S ALIVE!

1. Dr S. built Frankie with nuts and bolts, but you'll need paper and a pencil. Start by drawing a wonky rectangle.

2. Add an egg shape for the right foot, a semicircle for the left foot and a rectangle for the head.

3. Divide both the head and body rectangles in two. Add lines with large circles at the end for the arms and hands.

4. Create an arch between the two feet for Frankie's legs. Add fingers and eyes and then start the bolts that hold his head in place.

5. Give Frankie some hair and a face. Finish the bolts and the tattered edge of his shirt.

6. Stitches show where his head was cut open to insert the brain. Pupils in different positions show he's only just come to life! Eureka!

HERE CHICKY CHICKY!

1. Igor's pet, Chickenstein, starts life as a triangle with curved corners.

2. Add an oval on the left and a semicircle on the right then draw curves around them, make sure you leave a big gap.

3. Two circles on the top of the triangle form his googly eyes. Add five fingers between the ovals and the curves to form his hand-wings!

4. You can erase the extra lines on his hand-wings now. Next, add a triangular beak and two short legs.

5. Fingernails and feet come next, then three circles for his comb.

Design a new creature by joining up odd body parts!

6. Stitches hold his hands in place and a cloud of dust suggests he's on the run, maybe he's trying to escape from the lab!

CREATE YOUR OWN MONSTER FROM THESE BODY PARTS!

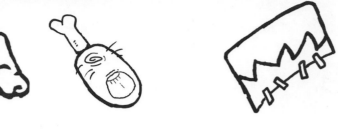

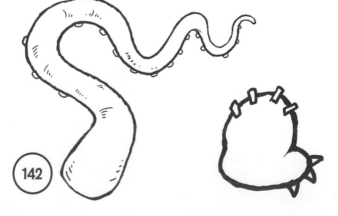